THE COAST
IS CLEAR

POEMS BY
MATT AMOTT

Top Shelf Poetry Series #2

Six Ft. Swells Press

After Hours Poetry

The Coast Is Clear

Copyright 2012 © Matt Amott

Top Shelf Poetry Series #2
Six Ft. Swells Press
Grass Valley, CA 95945
www.AfterHoursPoetry.com
sixfootswells@yahoo.com
Facebook: Six Ft. Swells Press

Editors: Todd Cirillo, Julie Valin
Cover Photo by The Capt. c/o Six Ft. Swells Photo Dept.
Photo Model: Alexis Corso
Book & Cover Design: Julie Valin, The Word Boutique,
www.TheWordBoutique.net

Acknowledgements:
Some of these poems have appeared in Red Fez; Rattlesnake
Review; NCPS Anthology; Primal Urge; Tonight You're Coming
Home With Us; Savage Melodies & Last Call Serenades; Desired
Destination; and Book Stack Coffee Table.

Gratitude:
The hard-working staff at the Six Ft. Swells home office.
Copy Right and Kinko's for helping with those early chapbooks.
The numerous towns, trains and taverns that supplied the
setting for my poems, and the people with whom I shared a
drink, a song, a story, or a night that supplied the themes for
my poems.

A special thanks for the wanderlust that won't leave me
alone...nor do I want it to.

ISBN 13: 978-0-9853075-0-9
ISBN 10:   0985307501

To
those that broke my heart,
those who mended it,
and those who
never took a chance.

Mile Markers

Keep On Truckin'

It is only fitting that when I sit down to write this introduction, I have a glass of Jack Daniels and a mix of Son House, Sam Cooke, Rebirth Brass Band, John Lee Hooker, Mississippi John Hurt and Black Sabbath playing from my stereo. It is as if my bags are already packed and I'm on my way to anywhere, confident that I will meet Matt at a Happy Hour somewhere along the way. That is the raw, hands-on experience that the reader gets from the poems in *The Coast is Clear*.

This collection is all about waiting for that sign: the light on in the bedroom window, tie on the door, a barroom napkin with a lipstick phone number, two quick raps on the door, the smell of perfume or cologne that is not yours. Signs that tell you it is time. Time to move on, write a poem, hit the road, or make your move. It is a cross-country diesel-humming search for that beacon cutting through the darkness, and Matt finds it every time.

These poems are lighthouses, pubs, potential, blues, Saturday nights, walks in the rain, thunderstorms, broke down cars, busted hearts, train tracks, promises, jukeboxes and hopeful first or even fourth chances. It is a collection of lust-filled melodies and broken guitar-string blues, roadside attractions and pay-by-the-hour motels. It takes us to towns we always wanted to visit, trains we wanted to hop, kisses we wish took place, or hoped would have never ended.

Matt writes of knowing when to take the necessary action required of the moment. Sometimes that action is as simple as "I'm gone." And that is the crux of it all...having the whiskey fortitude to pack it all up or shut it all down, understanding that, as Waylon Jennings sings, "all the places must be better than the ones we've left behind." Matt's poems take us miles upon miles, word by word.

So hop aboard, it's time to move—the coast is clear.

- Todd Cirillo, poet, editor
3/13/12 12:27a.m.

Lighthouse

When her date goes
to the bar
to refill drinks,
she turns
to me
and smiles.
Her blue eyes shine
across the room,
the way the lighthouse
signals a ship
that the coast is clear.

Product Placement

The beautiful redhead
works
the register,
while I stand
in the checkout line
eyeing
the magazines
and Tootsie Pops.

I finally give in
and ask for
her number,
another sucker
for the
impulse buy.

Insomniac

Just off a 12-hour shift
on a crappy Monday
his car won't start,
so he walks the miles home
with heavy steps.

He passes the bar
with dollar drafts
and a tied ball game,
but he's not interested
tonight.

6 hours
before his next shift
he longs for sleep.

He's not even through the door
before he drops everything,
a trail of clothes
follow him to his bed.
He eases
under the sheets,
alarm set,
lights out.

The phone rings,
it's her.

"I can't sleep," she says,
"can you talk for a bit?"

"Sure," he says.
"I wasn't tired
anyway."

Haircut

She saw her hair
as a distraction,
so she cut it short.

Now,
when I kiss
her neck,
the goose bumps
have nowhere
to hide.

The Mirage

Days drinking
in the desert heat,
lead to nights
howling
at the moon
and galaxies
far away.

By daybreak
I am back
by the pool,
howling
into a glass
of dark
bourbon whiskey,
reminding me
of the night sky
and for a brief moment
I forget
the hundreds of miles
that separate
you
from me.

"Otis: Live At The Whiskey"

Friday night,
me and the boys gather
at the hut before heading out
to conquer the evening.

Checks cashed,
wallets overflow
and drinks mixed
as Otis Redding
on the turntable
cries away

the last grip
of a nine to five
work week.

One night
of reckless abandon,
two days
to recover...

I like the odds.

The crew spills out
into the city early
to take advantage
of happy hour.

Bars, taverns, pubs & dives
line the row,
we stride with confidence.

The streets haven't
yet filled with regrets,
only potential.

Grazing

I read
her books
at night,
when
I'm wanting
and alone.
Her seductive words,
so fearless,
jump
from the page
and wrap themselves
around my head,
just where
I want her
legs
to be.

Nice Manners

She catches me
watching her
closely.

Walking away,
her hips offer
an extra swagger
in tight jeans—

a
nice
introduction.

Are You Still Mine?

(Righteous Brothers)

I sit
in the booth,
waiting for her
to walk
into the diner.

She left
days ago
to break it off
with him.

She said
I was
worth it.

So every night
I sit here,
waiting.

After closing
I walk home
to my place alone,
where the radio
pleads
"I'll be comin'
home,
wait for me,"

and I leave
the locks
unchained.

Eclipse

The morning train's
gonna take her
away. . .

So their last night
is spent
in each other's arms
on a window sill
high above the city,
lost in the stars
that reflect
in their eyes.

Below them,
a streetlight shines
upon an old man
with a guitar
who sings
"Sun,
don't you rise
no more."

Car Troubles

Every night
it was her,
that drove me
to the liquor store.

We didn't
even own
a car.

Holding Hands

The drive home
will take a few hours.
She is quiet,
and he watches
her stare out
the window
into the night.

He asks
if she had
a good time,
she slides over
and grabs his hand
that rests
between them.

Her fingers trace
the shape,
caressing his
weathered skin
and broken joints.

She kisses the scar
on his knuckle
and gently
moves his hand
under her dress
until his fingers
penetrate
her warmth,
heavy breaths pass
over her
bitten lip.

She says
that sometimes
the drive home
seems quicker,
and then leans
into his body
and whispers,

drive slower.

Testing the Lipstick

She was flirting
with the guy
across the room.
He was playing it
real cool
waiting for her
to approach him.
Before she made her move
she asked
if her lipstick was okay.
I said,
"let me check,"
and planted
a long kiss on her lips.
I withdrew,
told her
her lipstick was fine
and turned to order.

When she caught her breath
the guy was a memory
and I had already ordered
drinks for two.

On A Sunny Afternoon

She always kept track
of the unusual places
that we
kissed.

#6 was at the heavy metal show
covered in fake blood
as the band roared on,
#7 was soon to follow.

#4 was at the Blue Lamp
admiring the artwork
on the back wall
as the cowpunks crowded
the stage and cheered
every time Joe Buck called
them *motherfuckers!*

#3 took place
surrounded by
bulging pecks, deltoids
and quads
courtesy of free tickets
to a body building competition.

#1—
after frozen yogurt
downtown,
approaching sirens
wailed,
looking for the smoke
we left behind.

Dear John

I wrote
dozens
of letters
to win
your heart.

You wrote
only one
to break
mine.

Urban Jukejoint

I write poems
in my little apartment,
situated in the middle
of the city.

My blues records
play at full volume
through headphones
that lay on the floor.

The distorted
slide guitar
of *Black Snake Moan*
sounds distant,
as it blends
with the wind
that blows outside
my window
and harmonizes
with the whistle
that departs
Sacramento station.

I'd like to think
that this is how it would sound
if I was passed out
drunk in a field
outside of Junior's Place
in Hollis Springs,
Mississippi,

on any goddamned
Saturday
night.

Stolen Kiss

He's running late
so she moves down
to the empty barstool
next to mine.

We ramble on
for hours
our heads floating
in a sea of whiskey,
ranting and raving
like two mad souls
reunited to share
tales of long journeys
never to be separated
again.

As she waits,
she kisses a cocktail napkin
to remove the excess
lust from her lips.

Then he arrives
and the gaze we held
is gone.

Daylight fades,
long shadows
creep into the bar
and the Cowboy Junkies
sigh *Blue Moon*
on the jukebox.

As I leave
I set the mouth of my empty glass
over her red lips
stained
on a cocktail napkin
to capture
a kiss
that never belonged
to me.

Hope Sandoval Sings My Blues

It started raining
as she and I sat
in the car.
Mazzy Star played
on the radio
while she told me
I wasn't the one
she loved.

Exiting the vehicle
into the storm,
an outbound
whistle
sounds—

a beacon
for the
wayward
and
broken-hearted.

Rekindled

Never thought
I would see
her again,
until there
she stood.

10 years
of wondering,
gone,

the moment
our lips
first met
in the parking lot
on a Thursday—

better
late
than
never.

Explaining The Situation

The poet told me
to write more
short poems.

I heeded his advice
when I wrote
my woman
a poem
that read:

I'm gone.

Perks

I wake early
on a summer morning,
lone sheet
covers our bodies.
Her breasts
rise and fall
in the sunlight
as she breaths.

I reach over her
to open the window
light breeze sweeps across,
her nipples perk
against the sheet
in the cool morning air,

a reminder
to finish reading
Henry Miller.

Dessert

I always arrive
at the diner
after midnight,
when I know
she will be
working.

She hears
the keys jingle
on my belt
as I take
the corner booth.

She walks over,
says,
"I knew
it was you
without looking,"
and then sits
down next to me,
quietly whispers *hi*
and smiles,
placing her hand
on my thigh—

the cherry
on top
before I even order
dessert.

The Perfect Death

She called from the city
to say she missed me.

We talked for hours
in the stillness of the night
until her phone died
around 3 am.

When I see her
I express my regret in
killing her phone.

She says,

"don't apologize,
its final moments
were spent listening
to your words
whispered
in my ear."

It was the perfect death.

Strongly Worded Letter

He sits alone at the bar
next to an empty chair
that was supposed to be
for her.

A bottle of Old Crow
sits between two glasses—
one empty
and one emptied
many times.

He re-reads the letter
that said she wasn't coming,

something about
if it's too good
to be true,
it probably is.

He pulls out a wad of cash
and lays it on the bar

asking the barkeep
for something
from the top shelf.

The barkeep asks,
"You need something stronger?"

Yeah,
the Crow alone
can't carry away
the memory of her.

First Wave

You were like
my first wave
lifting me to new heights
and speeds
that had me fearing
for my life,
engulfing me
throwing me
end over end
pushing and pinning
me to the bottom.

Years later,
when I saw you
heading to the beach,
I picked up my board
and went home.

I've had my fill
of swimming
with sharks.

Let's Go Trippin'

(quotes by KC)

She only arrived
in the Northwest
a few months back.
Leaving the tropical islands
with a broken suitcase
and a broken heart
from a cheating
scoundrel.

My request for a date
denied, again and again.
She hated the cold,
suffered homesick, sadness
and insisted on being
acquaintances
as long as the winter
rain drowned her soul.

Then I showed up
at her place
with a heat lamp,
Dick Dale records,
salt and tequila.
We indulged
in margaritas
and dancing all afternoon
'til the supplies ran low.

I knew her
heart thawed, when
"for want of salt,
she licked
my neck".

New Day

You said
you've had it,
and walked away
like the last flash
of the evening sunset,

only to rise
the next morning
from ruffled sheets
beside me.

Expectations

She included me
in her book
of erotic poems.

Now the pressure
is on
to live up to
her expectations.

What will she think
as I wrap
my arm around her waist
pressing my tension
against her?

Will she enjoy
lingering kisses
on her neck
while I remove
the straps
of her dress?
And tolerate
a soft nibble
upon
raised nipples?

Not to mention,
a curious tongue
around her thighs,

penetrating
moist lips
until all
her synapses
are firing?

That's
a good start I think,
or
she can
re-read her poem
on how
I was supposed
to do it.

Citation

Her and I
play hooky
and go to the city
for the day.
We sit on the lawn
in the park,
talking, laughing,
sneaking sips
out of paper bags
so the cops
won't see us.

On our way out,
we pass two of them
on bikes.
I walk slowly
so the empty bottles
in my pack
don't clink together.
It's a heavy fine
to drink in public.

We cross the street
to a burger joint.
She walks in front of me
and my eyes drift down,
admiring how her
jeans wrap tight
around her hips.

I look up to see
her eyes reflected
in the glass window,
watching me
watch her.

She smiles,
knowing
if they don't catch you
for one thing,
they catch you
for another.

Desired Destination

The message
on the machine was clear:

she ran into an
old flame
while on the trip—
her first true love.
What are the odds?

I promised to pick her up
at the train station,
watched them kiss
on the platform.

Nearby
a mighty
Santa Fe
grinds
to a halt
while
my heartbreak
rumbles on,
knowing
I am not
her
desired
destination.

Snowed In

After five minutes
of silence
she uncrossed her arms
and walked out
into the season's first blizzard.

I finished my beer
and waited
for the snow plow.

I have never seen
such a cold front
come into town

and leave the room

at the exact same time.

Zephyr

Standing on the platform
watching the train roll to a stop,
The locomotive massive,
bright, shiny, silver,
like an old Airstream trailer
the folks would load
with their belongings,
and drag across the country
looking for a brighter future.

I see its strength
in sleek lines
running up the side
all the way to the front.

The engineer views the world
through windows
resembling squinting eyes
that are forever closed to slits,
drawn tight from looking at miles
of desert plains and rocky grades.

I make my way down a string of cars
until a weathered old man
with a pocket watch
and a lifetime of railroad stories asks,
      "Are you Chicago bound?"
      My reply, a nod.
      "Well son, hop on board."

    And that's
      as simple
        as it gets
          to just leave.

The Longest Night

Winter solstice—
the longest night,

more time
to ramble
and laugh,
more time
for another bottle,
another smoke,
and to sit in the bed
of the truck
holding your hand
a little longer
while the stars
slow down
to watch
our smiles.

The Last Poem I'll Write

Alone in the bar
beyond last call,
the bartender
likes my stories
and my face,
so she lets me finish my drink.
She even pours one for herself
and we toast
the moon and stars
that will guide us tonight.

All my friends
have gone home
to their wives
and husbands,
and the city boys
have come up and swept
all of the pretty girls
off their feet.

The jukebox
plays its last quarter
to a lonely room
filled with memories
of whiskey soaked tales,
wild romance
& crushed hearts.

I tip her a twenty
with a promise
to send
a postcard.

A kiss goodbye
and her smile
lets me know
I've already become
a bar story,
a legend
she will tell
fondly
over the years.

It warms me
as I walk away
into the night
to live
my own
myth.

No Maps Needed

I long to roam
like days past,

a beast exploring
the urban Serengeti
of the northern continent.

To look for that neon
welcome sign
in the shape
of a martini glass,
to drink old whiskey
in a new bar.

To drag the prettiest
lady in the room,
onto the dance floor
and hoof it until the band
blows the roof off the place.
Then lay naked
in her bed,
kissing her neck
and whispering
blush-filled poems
in her ear.

To pack a car
with wine and song.
No maps needed—
I know the way
by heart
to get wherever it is
I'm going.

Matt Amott's turn-ons: pre-1978 custom
Dodge vans, OP/Lightning Bolt apparel, shirts
with numbers, cords, heavy fuzz, deep Blues,
heart-wrenching Soul, record players, CB radios,
postcards, Kung Fu movies, Logan's Run,
hitchhiking, patches/iron-ons, and longboards.

He is also pretty friendly.

Made in the USA
Charleston, SC
26 April 2012